Michael Gow's

Away

Study notes for Area of Study:
Discovery
2015–2018 HSC

Maree Jones

A
FIVE SENSES
PUBLICATION

Five Senses Education Pty Ltd
2/195 Prospect Highway
Seven Hills 2147
New South Wales
Australia

First Published 2014

Jones, Maree
Top Notes – Away
ISBN 978 -1- 74130 – 989 – 8

CONTENTS

TOP NOTES SERIES

This series has been created to assist HSC students of English in their understanding of set texts. Top Notes are easy to read, providing analysis of issues and discussion of important ideas contained in the texts.

Particular care has been taken to ensure that students are able to examine each text in the context of the module it has been allocated to.

Each text generally includes:

- Notes on the specific module
- Plot summary
- Character analysis
- Setting
- Thematic concerns
- Language studies
- Essay questions and a modelled response
- Other textual material
- Study practice questions
- Useful quotes

We have covered the areas we feel are important for students in their study of Discovery for their Area of Study. I am sure you will find these Top Notes useful in your studies of English.

Bruce Pattinson
Series Editor

AREA OF STUDY: DISCOVERY

'We learn wisdom from failure much more than from success. We often discover what will do, by finding out what will not do; and probably he who never made a mistake never made a discovery.'

SAMUEL SMILES

The Area of Study set for the 2015–18 HSC is *Discovery*. It is compulsory to study this topic as prescribed by the Board of Studies. Remember you are supposed to analyse your texts with reference to varying aspects of *Discovery*. Markers will be looking to see evidence of deep conceptual understanding of the Area of Study and you are encouraged to support your views with close textual referencing.

In the Area of Study you will be analysing many texts that are related to the idea of discovery. You will analyse texts not only to investigate the ideas they present about this area but also how they deliver these ideas. This means you will be looking closely at the techniques composers use to represent ideas and shape meaning. You will also be looking at relationships between texts. Overall, you will become an expert on discovery- the different notions people have about it and the various ways composers manipulate techniques to communicate their ideas about the topic. The material in this Top Note will help you do that.

Specifically you will look at:

- A set text from the following list of fourteen texts. **You will only study one of these.**
  - *Wrack* – James Bradley
  - *The Awakening* – Kate Chopin
  - *A Short History of Nearly Everything* – Bill Bryson
  - *The Motorcycle Diaries* – Ernesto 'Che' Guevara
  - *Swallow the Air* – Tara June Winch
  - *Away* – Michael Gow
  - *Rainbow's End* – Jane Harrison
  - *Frank Hurley - The Man Who Made History* – Simon Nasht
  - *Life of Pi* – Ang Lee
  - *The Tempest* – William Shakespeare
  - *Selected Poems* – Robert Gray
  - *Selected Poems* – Rosemary Dobson
  - *Selected Poems* – Robert Frost
  - *Go Back To Where You Came From* – selected episodes – Ivan O'Mahoney
- Additional related texts of your own choosing.

You must write about your set text and additional texts of your own choosing in the first English paper of the HSC examination.

I hope that posterity will judge me kindly, not only as to the things which I have explained, but also to those which I have intentionally omitted so as to leave to others the pleasure of discovery.

RENE DESCARTES

WHAT DOES THE BOARD OF STUDIES REQUIRE FOR THE AREA OF STUDY?

The Board of Studies documentation says of the Area of Study: Discovery that it;

'requires students to explore the ways in which the concept of discovery is represented in and through texts.' (p 9)

The document English Stage 6 Prescriptions: Area of Study Electives and Texts (August 2013) notes that perceptions of discovery can encompass many things and are shaped by context.

- Students can consider –not only discovery but also rediscovery.
- That discovery may be planned or unplanned and may lead to new worlds and values.
- Discoveries can question and challenge and lead to different conclusions.

You will also need to consider that the 'process of discovering can vary according to personal, cultural, historical and social contexts and values.'

Below is an abbreviated version of what the Board requires of students.

'In their responses and compositions students examine, question, reflect and speculate on':

- their own experiences of discovery, personally and through texts.

- the assumptions underlying the representations of discovery.
- the effects of composers' choices of techniques.
- the ways in which the study of discovery has helped them understand the world and themselves.

Think carefully about the wording that is used so that you can adopt this language for your own work.

If this is what is required by the Board of Studies you need to examine the concept of discovery carefully so you can respond adequately. We would recommend that you read the complete document which is on the Board of Studies website (http://www.bostes.nsw.edu.au) and can be downloaded in Word or PDF formats.

UNDERSTANDING THE AREA OF STUDY

'There is no better high than discovery'

- E. O. WILSON

Discovery is often associated with adventure. The word *Discovery* conjures childhood dreams of exotic locations, intrepid explorers in jungles discovering lost tribes and great treasures. Movies embrace this theme. The Discovery Channel exists to help people to discover facts vicariously. The concept behind the never-ending Star Trek series is to 'explore strange new worlds, to seek out new life and new civilisations, to boldly go where no man has gone before'.

Even the self-discovery / self-help industry is a major one in all the nations of earth; people are willing to make great sacrifices to discover the 'truth' about themselves and the world. All this is undoubtedly true but discovery is much more than this and we will need to have a broader and more sophisticated understanding to undertake our studies of the texts set for study.

The Board of Studies has outlined in their documentation: students are required to 'explore the ways in which the concept of discovery is represented in and through texts'. (p 9 *HSC Prescriptions 2015–20 English Stage 6*). This is our first step and it indicates that we must pay particular attention to the text and its content and techniques, particularly the techniques the composer uses to engage the audience and convey the main purpose of their text.

The whole aim of this Area of Study is to examine the text closely but also relate it to the idea of discovery and decide how examining it in this way enables us to better understand both the text and the concept. It is important that you formulate your own ideas about the text and attempt to develop some original and creative ideas about what you are studying.

The Board's documentation should be read in full and the annotations document should also be examined for the particular texts you are studying as this document offers insights into the way each particular text should be examined by outlining key ideas and areas for clarification.

The *Prescriptions* document states on the Area of Study that *Discovery* can be:

- something new
- a rediscovery
- sudden, unexpected
- carefully planned
- 'fresh and intensely meaningful in ways that may be emotional, creative, intellectual, physical and spiritual.' (p9)

- confronting
- provocative
- enable speculation

It can:

- change perceptions of individuals and groups.
- create new values

The document also suggests that discoveries and ways of discovering vary due to individual circumstance and that these discoveries can change many things about lives, communities and the world(s). Of course when we examine the concept of discovery we need to examine how 'discovering' the text itself may change us and how we view things. The text may challenge and confront and change how we see the human experience.

Students can also think about 'their own experiences of discovery' and how a composer's choice of form, feature and language influences their views of discovery. Examining and enjoying any text is a discovery in itself but it is what we take away from the text and apply that is the real discovery. That is not to say that every text will be enjoyed or offer a discovery. Some may not personally engage you and that is fine. This is especially so when you begin to find other related material that links to Discovery. Find examples of texts that link in significant ways to your prescribed text.

Defining Discovery

'Definition is the death of discovery'

-TOM SHADYAK

Now let's define discovery in a more coherent and easily understood way so we can begin our investigation at a basic level before moving into more complex analysis. Dictionary.com defines the term as:

1. The act or instance of discovering
2. Something discovered
3. In legal terms it is compulsory disclosure of evidence
4. The name of the third space shuttle.

Obviously the first three terms are more suitable but the final definition shows how pervasive the idea of discovery is and how it has influenced people over time. The search for the 'new' has driven much development over past millennia. Discoveries are always met with excitement and often trepidation as to what change they might bring.

Think historically about how people have reacted to change. It can cause great upheavals in society, with violent reactions while other changes brought through discoveries are welcomed and may save and enhance lives. Consider medical advancements, scientific developments and the ever-quickening world of the computer. Even the way I am creating this text in Evernote on an iPad would not have been possible twelve months ago. Discovery brings change and may affect different people or groups of people, even nations in various ways both positive and negative. It is pertinent now to examine some more definitions.

The word discover and its definition also sheds some light on the concept:

1. To see, get knowledge, to learn, to find, get knowledge of something previously seen or unknown.

As does the definition of the word discovering:

1. Noticing or realising.

These definitions all point to the fact that realisation is the key to discovery. This realisation may come unexpectedly, occasionally or never. Someone else may have the same experience and make the discovery. The realisation may be accidental or organised, take years in the planning or come as a complete surprise.

Discoveries can come in many ways and the synonyms for discover listed below help us to understand the concept even further. They assist in defining how a discovery can arise:

Synonyms – ascertain, catch, come upon, contrive, determine, design, dig up, disclose, elicit, explore, bring to light, unearth, encounter, experiment, invent, originate, expose, locate, perceive, sense, strike, verify.

These synonyms show partly the vast array of words that our language has created around this concept and show how important it is in the human psyche. Look also at the antonyms that show how we view not discovering things; lose, miss, pass by.

We, as a race, want to discover. Now we will look at some examples of discovery and examine their impact. It is also important to remember that discoveries do not have to be positive. You might discover you have a huge problem, an incurable illness, a strange past, an unwelcome relative or something equally bizarre. There may be a darker side to any discovery that could be addressed. Think about the effect of the white discoverers on indigenous populations.

Types of Discovery

Personal Discovery

'I think a spiritual journey is not so much a journey of discovery. It's a journey of recovery. It's a journey of uncovering your own inner nature. It's already there.'

BILLY CORGAN

The idea of personal discovery or self-discovery as many of the books also describe it, is a popular and pervasive concept. It is more prevalent in the developed nations of the world where people seek something more spiritual or meaningful rather than their consumer driven lives and the day to day grind of work. Many seek something more; they strive to discover something within or without, a better self, a way to live in the now or just a way to escape from reality. A huge amount of material (literature, DVDs, audiobooks) has been assembled to help individuals achieve their life goals.

Individuals seek to achieve personal discovery in a variety of ways. Some examples are courses and conferences where they are led through exercises, both physical and psychological, to develop new skills and discover their inner spirituality. Others join communities, religious groups or renounce material possessions and become itinerant travellers or, in old fashioned terms, 'hippies'. Through this they discover whatever they lack in their current state (hopefully) and become a better or more effective person. Others use these discoveries to enrich themselves or manage better in their existing lives. Whatever the reason or outcome, personal discovery is a huge industry and an integral part of our society.

For more information on this area you could investigate the self-help, self- improvement section of a book store or get on YouTube and type these terms in. You will get plenty of ideas and advice!

Inner Discovery

'The greatest discovery of my generation is that man can alter his life simply by altering his attitude of mind.'

JAMES ADAMS

The concept of inner discovery is closely aligned with the previous topic and can be seen similarly yet it is more aligned with exceptional circumstances. For example some people learn much about themselves during physical, emotional or psychologically stressful times and are astounded by the inner strength they have while others around them break down or fail to cope. Others find inner strength through meditation, retreats, or extremes such as becoming a hermit and focusing on the inner person. This concept of personal enlightenment is also a business in the modern world and you can get coaches who will work with you to find your inner self through various processes of discovery.

If you are looking for examples to use in your related material try googling the term and you will find a whole range of programs, coaches and books that will help you find your inner self. Dag Hammarskjold (former UN Secretary General) said 'The longest journey is the journey inwards. Of him who has chosen his destiny, who has started upon his quest for the source of his being.'

Discovery through Travel

The idea of discovery through travel is one of the first things that occur to people when they hear the word discovery. As Martin Buber (Austrian-born 20th Century Jewish philosopher) stated, 'All journeys have secret destinations of which the traveller is unaware'. This sense of travel enabling discoveries is well documented and became even more prominent as people began to sail widely across the seas to discover 'new' lands, many of which had been occupied by indigenous peoples for centuries. Travel was, and to some extent still is, associated with an adventure, a journey, to test the boundaries of what we already know and to see how far we can take the new experience and how it changes us. What we discover on our travels is revealing and often confronting.

> *Adventure is a path. Real adventure—self-determined, self-motivated, often risky—forces you to have firsthand encounters with the world. The world the way it is, not the way you imagine it. Your body will collide with the earth and you will bear witness. In this way you will be compelled to grapple with the limitless kindness and bottomless cruelty of humankind—and perhaps realise that you yourself are capable of both. This will change you. Nothing will ever again be black-and-white.*
>
> – **MARK JENKINS**
>
> (HTTP://MATADORNETWORK.COM/BNT/50-MOST-INSPIRING-TRAVEL-QUOTES-OF-ALL-TIME/#RCM3GIDFT04P07MB.99)

Discovery through travel brings this kind of change and it may involve understanding another culture, disrupting a prejudice or habit, making a friend or discovering some amazing natural beauty. Discovery through travel is one of the most written about and frequently mentioned ideas when discussing the concept. Travel has certainly changed over the centuries, even in the past decade travel to distant places has become commonplace. Air travel has especially become less than the special thing for the privileged or extremely adventurous that it was in the beginning. Think back to the times when to travel from place to place by foot or by horse was a major event. From the Middle Ages through to the later eighteenth century many people had never ventured beyond their village, apart from an infrequent trip to the nearest town. This idea leads us to consider the idea of the journey.

Discovery through Journey

This is an idea common to many areas of the discovery concept. Often the two words are associated if we think of the journey as a process not just a physical movement. Often discoveries are made on the journey rather than at the destination. The word journey has also been applied to abstract concepts. Lyndon Johnson, the American President, described peace as a deliberate process: 'Peace is a journey of a thousand miles and it must be taken one step at a time'. Many have heard the quote by Lao Tzu 'A journey of a thousand miles must begin with one step'.

The concept of journey leading to discovery is a constant in modern film and literature and it has been extensively studied in works such as Joseph Campbell's *The Hero's Journey*. This model organises the journey by stages which are common to all culture. Despite the cross-cultural commonalities, journeys allow discovery about self and such discoveries are individual.

As Marcel Proust (19th and 20th Century French novelist) stated, 'We don't receive wisdom; we must discover it for ourselves after a journey that no one can take for us or spare us.'

The physical journey could be local, in the same country, overseas or even in space, a place many science fiction texts take us. Fantasy writers create journeys of discovery in worlds of imagination and invention. Film also focuses on the concept of discovery through journey as we see in the range of road trip movies that seem so appealing to teen audiences. More serious films examine personal independence, the human condition and how one can discover something on the journey that will change or even save humanity. You will find many examples of this in film but try and choose something where the discovery has some significant personal and/or social impact and you can discuss techniques. Consider the idea of the journey as being inextricably linked to the concept of discovery as you make your way through the Area of Study.

Scientific and Technological Discovery

'Scientists have become the bearers of the torch of discovery in our quest for knowledge'

STEPHEN HAWKING

Regarding areas of discovery, foremost in many people's thoughts are the breakthroughs made in science and technology. They have immediate and significant impacts on modern day individuals and the way they interface with the world.

Examples of the impact of technology include:

- increased internet usage leading to the rise of social networking.
- miniaturisation of hand-held devices such as the iPad enabling people to communicate easily and more often.

- rapid changes in the way that data is stored such as the increased use of cloud-storage services has facilitated the development of much more flexible devices.

Einstein pointed out 'The process of scientific discovery is, in effect, a flight from wonder.' This is central to much of the debate that has raged over science in the past century or so. How do we progress scientifically and technologically and still maintain a moral and ethical basis? Should we chase many of the ideas that have arisen? For example the machines of war, the chemicals that kill and the genetic manipulations that can lead to social engineering are discoveries with ethical implications. Should there be limits and controls and if so how much? Discoveries can be fraught with danger on many levels.

While it is part of discovery to imagine and test the boundaries and seek new ways, it is also probably integral to human nature. With these new technologies the consequences are even greater than in the past as more people can be affected, more invasively and quickly. Dangers emerge as people discover new methods of being destructive, such as invading computers to distort programs with viruses or stealing through cybercrimes. These examples highlight that discoveries are not always positive.

Humanity must also grapple with the discovery of things such as climate change and environmental issues that are the result of industrialisation through discovered technologies. The consequences of many of the discoveries in the latter half of the last century are still being felt and new discoveries are needed to solve these problems. Discovery can be cyclical, inter-related and never-ending. Google '2014 Shift Happens' and watch a YouTube clip highlighting the rapid rate of discovery and change in this modern era!

Discovery as Creating New From Old

This is an intriguing idea probably best summed up in the idea of recycling materials to create something new. Old tyres can be used as soft fall for children's playgrounds, old ideas can be given new form, new ways can be thought up to approach a topic. Even just drawing attention to a common feature can enable people to discover something about it. This form of discovery is seen as creativity.

One example might be the light show Vivid which featured in Sydney. Prominent buildings such as the Opera House were illuminated with an exciting coloured light show. The buildings around the harbour foreshores were visible and bathed in psychedelic colours. People flocked to see the spectacle and the show received great reviews. The reactions evoked by the light show captured the idea of discovery and re-invention as otherwise familiar images were seen in an entirely new way. The sense of wonder and amazement experienced by young children observing the show was evidence of their discovery.

Sometimes a newly discovered thing can be as simple as reading a novel previously read or re-watching a film seen years before and getting something new or different from it. Great artists always borrow from the past and rearrange old elements into new discoveries for their audiences. Ideas such as this have led to new movements in the Arts or new methods of approaching a topic that casts new light on it. Postmodern texts such as the film *The Matrix*, use intertextuality as a key aspect.

Learning as Discovery

Learning in itself is a discovery that can make significant changes to an individual or a group. When we learn something that can be applied it is a small but potentially significant discovery for the individual or group. One significant piece of learning was the manipulation of fire, another the growing of crops, developing shelter and so on. While these are major discoveries other learning can be especially important for the individual. One example might be a breakthrough in reading or the ability to analyse and manipulate information to create something new. Consider this aspect of discovery as it can link to the other areas and be useful as an overriding idea to utilise as a thesis for the Area of Study essay.

Detection as Discovery

> *The basis of drama is... The struggle of the hero toward a specific goal at the end of which he realises that what kept him from it was, in the lesser drama, civilisation and, in the greater drama, the discovery of something that he did not set out to discover but which can be seen retrospectively as inevitable.*
>
> **DAVID MAMET**

The concept of detection as discovery is the integral aspect of the success of the eternally popular crime fiction genre and is also a major aspect of thrillers and similar literature, film and the visual arts. Paintings, for example, prove excellent material, to demonstrate how an individual can deduce something different from the same work as the person next to them. Detection, however, in its truest form is highly valued by audiences as it is about discovering the truth through clues.

Much literature has been written in this quest to make sense of a world where justice sometimes appears to be lacking. Of course the detective genre has changed much over the years and these variations have come to suit changing audiences and contexts but this search has rarely varied despite the form in which it is presented. Audiences love the sense of discovery in detection and an examination of any television or film guide will attest to the fact, as will an examination of library bookshelves.

"HOLMES GAVE ME A SKETCH OF THE EVENTS."

The Psychology of Discovery

'There'll always be serendipity involved in discovery'

JEFF BUZOS

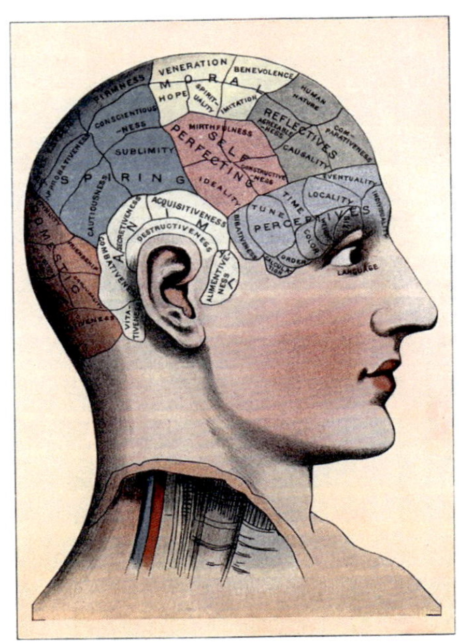

When I alluded to the innate need for discovery in the human psyche it wasn't superficial. The need for humanity to move ahead, to discover and to break boundaries is an important part of humanity's development and seems ingrained in us. The push to conquer new boundaries, to test, to push, to break boundaries is inherent in all development. Even if the discovery is the taste of a new food, the thrill of a new friend, or the discovery of any other sensory pleasure, it is a pleasure psychologically important to human development. The American writer Pearl S. Buck, who died in 1973, said that the basic discovery is the 'discovery of the relationship between men and women.' This is still true today. This quote could be used to explore the concept of discovery and to justify textual analysis from the perspective of feminist literary criticism. The field of Literary Criticism and new readings of texts is an example of boundary breaking.

There is something basic at an emotional level about discovery that attracts us to it. The new is important, broadening and thought provoking and this affects us on a psychological level. It is the emotional response that keeps people seeking the new, to discover and to absorb. This concept of the impact of discovery on our psyche is important as it is also a useful link to each of the texts and to your related material. It may be a useful concept to enable you to link your ideas together. Think about the basic psychological drives that motivate us and how they are important in all our discoveries.

Nationalism, Capitalism and other 'isms' as Drivers of Discovery

'People acting in their own self-interest is the fuel for all the discovery, innovation, and prosperity that powers the world'

JOHN STOSSEL

The idea that the 'isms' are drivers of discovery may not be appealing to some but there is no doubt that many of the discoveries of the last few centuries have been driven by them. One example is the race to land on the moon or the space race. This led to some awesome discoveries yet was driven by the great Cold War divide between the Communist Russian dictatorship and the American capitalist democratic system. Buoyed by the need to be first to set foot on the moon and discover what was there, billions were spent in making this happen.

Earlier still, the drive by nations such as Spain, Portugal and England to colonise the 'New World', particularly Africa and the Americas, led to many discoveries. National pride here was mixed with the drive for resources to support their ideology: religious, capitalist, communist or nationalist. This also led to many negatives such as exploitation in the race to conquer lands and spread 'civilisation'.

Capitalism, whatever your political belief, has been one of the greatest engines to drive discoveries over the centuries. This striving to produce product faster, more efficiently and thus, cheaply, has driven much innovation, prompted development of new technologies and resulted in new products. The instinct to improve and achieve is driven to its purest form by the capitalist system. It is not prudent here to discuss the pros and cons of the system itself but rather to recognise that it is a consummate motivator to Discovery. Gordon Gecko's quote from the film, *Wall Street*, sums up this philosophy brilliantly,

> *'Greed is right, greed works. Greed clarifies, cuts through and captures the essence of the evolutionary spirit. Greed in all of its forms; greed for life, for money, for love, knowledge has marked the upward surge of mankind.'*

Again relevant to this is the consideration of further analysing texts through the lens of literary criticism. For example, Marxist and New Historicist readings present different interpretations and may offer responders new insights and discoveries regarding texts.

Negative Aspects of Discovery

While it is common to have a positive image of discovery it is important to remember that it has negative aspects as well. For example, many of the early explorers who set out to discover new lands ended up dead. History is littered with such examples and many have gone down as glorious failures. One example is the story of Burke and Wills in Australia but you could also examine the exploration of the Antarctic and Arctic which have many failed expeditions. Other negatives can be found in the concept of discovering dreams of riches such as El Dorado or King Solomon's Mines.

The 'discovery' of new lands by European adventurers led to the exploitation of discovered natural resources. Indigenous peoples, considered uneducated savages, were often enslaved. The 'slave trade' was a negative by-product of this period of exploitation and discovery.

Away from this idea of exploration we can also have negatives in discoveries which yield promise such as nuclear power. This 'clean fuel' has been used for destructive purposes and Oppenheimer has said of his team's creation of the atomic bomb that it was a mistake. Many discoveries have been used negatively in war and in commerce for power and/or gain. We have even experienced psychological discoveries being used for brainwashing and other pernicious purposes. We have also mentioned the 'isms' that drive discovery and these can be negatively used as well. Communism killed millions and enslaved nations, patriotism in its extreme can lead to discovery but has impacted negatively on native populations and led to war.

Remember when you select a text for your related material or study a text there may be negatives to engage with that will enhance your understanding of the concept of discovery. Look for them to broaden your knowledge and ability to write clearly and formulate your own opinions.

Afterword on Discovery

'The pace of discovery is going unbelievably fast'

JAMES WATSON

Discovery is also about **possibility**, the idea that something in an imagination can be made real and attainable. Discovery is sometimes seeing the obvious and making use of it. Above all it entails faith/dreaming and an insatiable curiosity. When you read about many discoveries they are truly tales of failure with one success. Many stories tell of years of pain, toil, ridicule, dismal progress and rejection before success is achieved. Edison made a thousand bulbs before he got one to work. Failure is a constant with many people you will study in this topic until they discover their dream. They maintained their faith in the face of great adversity and this is what makes them discoverers. If it were easy everyone would do it!

Discoverers are also people who see what others have missed. Often they simply look at something in a new way. To look for new ideas, we must maintain an open mind. To discover for ourselves the mysteries of texts and how to unlock them, we must develop strategies for analysis and perseverance to achieve understanding.

Perhaps you think everything has been discovered as a pessimist might, but discoverers are optimists, people who continually seek success, or insight in achieving their goals or realising their dreams.

Questions for Discovery

- Define the term 'discovery' in your own words.
- How can discovery and possibility be connected?
- Discuss what the term discovery means to you.
- Create your own list of synonyms and antonyms for the word discovery. Then, choose two or three to use in your writing so the word discovery won't be repeated.
- Science is often connected with discovery. Research one such instance and write two paragraphs on it connecting it thematically to your set text.
- What is positive about discovery?
- Discuss the idea that discovery can be a two-edged sword.
- Discuss one discovery and the benefits of that discovery to humanity.
- Do you think the concept of discovery is integral to detective fiction? Explain your answer fully.
- Analyse one 'ism' and how discovery has been driven by it.
- Discuss some of the negatives associated with the concept of discovery.

STUDYING A DRAMA TEXT

The medium of any text is very important. If a text is a drama this must not be forgotten. Plays are not *read* they are *viewed*. This means you should never refer to the "reader" but the "audience" as the respondent to the text.

The marker will want to know you are aware of the text as a play and that you have considered its effect in performance.

Remembering a drama text is a play also means when you are exploring *how* the composer represents his/her ideas you MUST discuss dramatic techniques. This applies to any response you do using a drama, irrespective of the form the response is required to be in.

Dramatic techniques are all the devices the playwright uses to represent his or her ideas. They are the elements of a drama that are manipulated by playwrights and directors to make any drama effective on stage! You might also see them referred to as dramatic devices or theatrical techniques.

Every play uses dramatic techniques differently. Some playwrights are very specific about how they want their play performed on stage. Others like Shakespeare give virtually no directions. They might give detailed comments at the beginning of the play and/or during the script. These are usually in italics and are called *stage directions*. They are never spoken but provide a guide to the director and actors about how the play is to appear and sound when performed.

Some common dramatic techniques are shown on the diagram that follows.

DRAMATIC TECHNIQUES

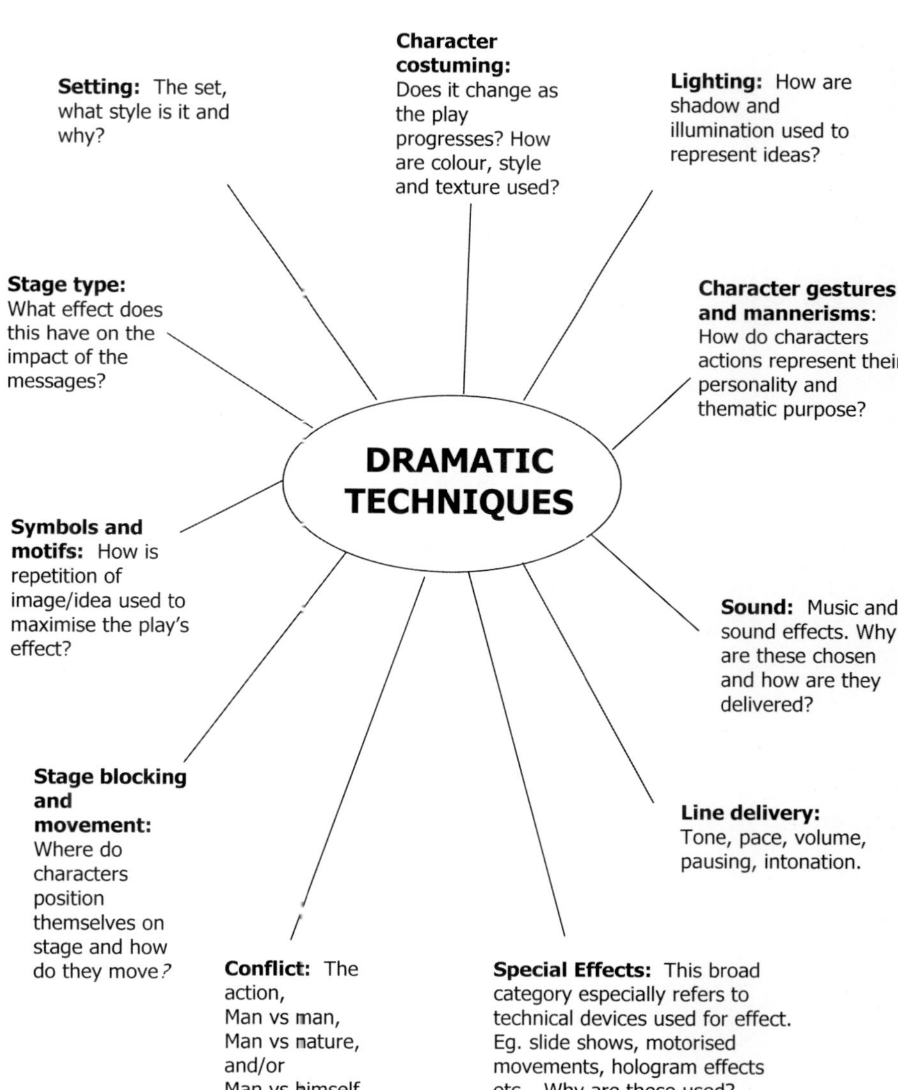

THE AUTHOR

Michael Gow (1955–) is an Australian playwright who has been involved in many other fields of entertainment. Obviously growing up in Australia during the time the play is set has influenced the work and the perspective he offers.

Gow has been involved in drama and related fields since around the age of fourteen when he acted and wrote for the Australian Young People's Theatre. He continued this work when, as a student at Sydney University, he acted in productions with the university drama society. Gow gained some overseas experience when he acted in England in the late 1970s.

After this experience he returned to Australia and gained a part in the film *Stir* in 1980. He then worked in television in shows such as *The Young Doctors* and *The Last Frontier.* He kept working in the theatre and had some lead roles around the country, giving him further valuable experience.

His first play, *The Kid*, was written in 1982 and has been performed around the country. He has had a one act play, The *Astronaut's Wife*, was produced and also made into a radio play. Gow has been quite prolific and wrote *Away* in 1986.

Away was an extremely successful play from the first and got excellent reviews and public acclaim. It has been produced many times throughout the country and has won numerous awards including the Premier's Literary Award for Best Play in 1986.

The fact that Gow was born and raised in Australia makes his settings and work peculiarly Australian and makes the characters representative of the country at that particular time and place. But the plays go beyond just being Australian; their thematic concerns are about relationships, communication, generational change and family life. *Away* is representative of this work that seems to have defied being categorised.

As an actor Gow has, as it were, been on the other side and his direction and writing show this experience. Other works by Gow include *Europe, Art 'n Life, 1841, On Top of the World* and *The Kid*.

CONTEXT OF THE PLAY

- Vietnam War
- Australia in the 1960s
- Leukaemia
- Mental illness
- Mendelssohn
- Shakespeare in the play

Vietnam War

The Vietnam War was fought initially between the French colonial powers and the communists supported by the Chinese and Russian regimes. The French had formed the Union of Indochina in 1893 and had become the dominating colonial power. They controlled the region until the Second World War.

After this communists, who wanted to rule all of Vietnam, controlled the north. The first Indochina War was fought between 1946 and 1954 and the Americans who rightly feared communist expansionism supported the French.

The French left after 1954 and the communists began to push into the free south in 1958. The South Vietnamese government appealed to America for help and as their allies we sent thirty advisers in 1962. Australia became involved because our government believed that the free world should help stop communist expansion.

In 1964 the government passed the National Service Act. This meant that twenty- year old men had to register and, if selected by a ballot, had to serve in the army. Australia then began to send more troops to help the South Vietnamese stay free. This is how Coral's son had been sent and killed. Roy's views are similar to the one's held by the leadership of the day. Rick's speech outlines the ballot system very well.

This led to a protest movement called the moratorium, by the Labor Party, trade unions, socialists, university students and other leftist groups. They marched in the streets and used civil disobedience because they thought the war was immoral.

Australia stopped conscription when the Labor Party won the 1972 election and we left Vietnam, which was subsequently overrun by communists. It was a war that had divided the country.

Australia in the 1960s

The play is set in the summer of 1967–68 and it moves around from the suburbs to the Gold Coast and the northern beaches. Australia was very different in the sixties and the campers are a good example of the prejudice that existed during the period. We see that they comment on 'the New Australian campers' and how they are different from 'proper Australian families'.

Remember that the dress and manners of the period were different and that the thinking was different. This is especially so of the older generation who had lived through the hard times of the depression. Many people were just beginning to recover from its effects. Gwen is an example of this.

Immigration was also becoming an issue with thousands of migrants coming from Europe for a better life here. Vic and Harry are examples of this type of migration and they are not always highly regarded. The Vietnam War was also an issue (see above). The country was also in an economic boom and Roy comments on our high standard of living.

Bramwell in the *Adelaide Review* (no. 46,1988 p.21) says

> *'The period is nominally the summer of 1967 – the Hippies' Summer of Love is better characterised by the language of anxiety and conflict than by pacifist platitudes. The War was marauding through young lives, feminism was finding a new voice for old grievances and Australia was no longer the favourite nephew of the Empire.'*

Development was also on a boom and the changes the campers want was also common as they did not have the huge legislative hurdles developers have now. There were also no environmental laws as Australia was still regarded as the lucky country.

Leukaemia

Leukaemia is a usually fatal disease, which is characterised by the excessive production of white blood cells. Some of the symptoms that accompany the disease are anaemia (lack of energy) and an increase in the size and activity of the spleen and Lymph glands.

This disease was incurable in the period the play is set and thus we know that Tom is doomed.

Mental Health

The attitudes to mental health have never been positive in our society and the institutionalisation of individuals with mental health problems has long been a solution. Often these institutions were more like jails except the inmates had fewer rights.

Mental illnesses comes in two main types, psychotic and non-psychotic. The psychotic illnesses are things like schizophrenia and manic depression while the non- psychotic are things such as anxiety attacks and obsessive compulsive disorder.

Individuals were institutionalised when they and/or their families could no longer cope with their behaviour. As time moved on things improved but they were still bleak in the 1960s and 70s in Australia. The policy was one of isolation and segregation from the community in psychiatric institutions. These did not have a good record of care and complaints from psychiatric patients could always be ignored as they may not be real.

Cases of physical and sexual abuse have been uncovered as have extensive use of electric shock and deep sleep therapy. Many of the staff were also under trained or not trained. Thus we can see why Coral would be concerned with the threat to lock her up and/or give her shock treatment. It is also understandable, in this context, that Roy would be ashamed of his wife.

Mendelssohn

Felix Mendelssohn was born at Hamburg in 1809 and died in 1847 aged thirty-eight. His music is considered romantic and non-theatrical. It is considered light and beautiful music. A child genius he was also a conductor before his early death.

A nocturne is a composition that suggests the romantic beauty of the night. It is usually a slow type of piano music and is music that is associated with the romantics. Mendelssohn wrote his nocturne for the scene in *A Midsummer Night's Dream* when Puck anoints the lover's eyes so they fall in love with the first person they see when they awake.

Shakespeare in the play

Two of Shakespeare's plays are mentioned in the quotations on the introductory page to the play. These are:

What country, friends is this? *Twelfth Night* Act 1, sc.ii.

I have done nothing but in care of thee,

Of thee, my dear one. *The Tempest*, Act 1 sc.ii.

Both these plays are Shakespearian comedies in which storms appear and change the course of people's lives. As comedies they have happy endings.

Two other plays feature in the play. They are *A Midsummer Night's Dream* and *King Lear. Away* begins with the final speech from *A Midsummer Night's Dream* spoken by Tom. This introduces the idea of fairies and that the audience shouldn't be offended by their silliness. It concludes happily with the idea that it was all a dream.

A speech from *King Lear* appears in the final scene and again Tom speaks it. In King Lear one character called Edgar is a loving son to the Earl of Gloucester. He takes the name Poor Tom in the play. This reflects the manner in which Tom helps Coral in the play.

King Lear is also about family relationships. It has as some of its issues the nature of family relationships, especially those of children with their parents. In *King Lear* there are other parallels with *Away*. One is the way that both young and old show their mortality. There is also a huge storm scene in *King Lear* and this is also replicated in this play.

Gow also uses the Shakespearian idea that conflicts are resolved and the natural order is again established. Other ideas he appropriates from Shakespeare are:

- Recognisable characters such as the nagging wife, young lovers and the henpecked husband.
- Soliloquies, for example Coral's exposition
- Fairies
- Storms
- The concept of the play within a play. e.g. 'The Stranger on the Shore'
- Multiple parts played by actors e.g. Roy/Hotel Guest/ First Camper/MC
- Mime e.g. Act Five Scene One
- Structure of Five acts

Gay in the article 'Michael Gow's Away: The Shakespeare Connection' in *Reconnoitres: Essays in Australian Literature* (1992 p204) writes,

> *'The play's Shakespearian references are integral to its structure, argument, and effect, but its strength lies equally in its rendering of the conditions and texture of modern Australian life'.*

Gow has integrated Shakespeare and made it relevant to modern Australian audiences.

PLOT OUTLINE

- We begin with the school play of Shakespeare's *A Midsummer Nights Dream*
- Roy talks to the audience and sets context – Christmas 1968
- Main characters are introduced in scene two and we learn they are all going on holidays
- Coral gives a short speech that defines her character – 'Alas'
- Harry and Tom talk about the coming holiday
- Gwen Meg and Jim prepare for their holiday
- Roy and Coral talk about their dead son, killed in the Vietnam War. They are off to the Gold Coast
- The families head off on holiday, each to their own destination
- Coral talks to Leonie and Rick
- Gwen tries to spoil Christmas
- Coral and Rick develop a relationship and Roy threatens her
- The storm happens, uniting two families and Coral has run away
- Gwen is transformed at the beach
- Tom asks Meg for sex
- The amateur concert is performed
- Penultimate scene is silent
- Tom reads the opening speech from King Lear

PLOT SUMMARY

ACT ONE

SCENE ONE

A school performance of Shakespeare's *A Midsummer Night's Dream* is taking place on stage and is near its end. Tom, a student at the school, gives the final speech from the play and the curtain closes.

The curtains open a little and the school Principal, Roy, appears and gives a speech to the audience. He talks about the play they have just seen, thanks all the people who helped and wishes everyone a happy Christmas for 1968.

QUESTIONS FOR ACT ONE SCENE ONE

- How does Gow establish the tone for the play by using the passage from Shakespeare's *A Midsummer Night's Dream*?
- How does Gow establish the time frame for the play in this scene?

SCENE TWO

Tom and Meg (Margaret), another student in the play, discuss going on holidays. Tom has bought her a present, a brooch, which he gives her. They begin to discuss the play and cannot seem to part even though they are struggling initially for conversation.

This conversation then turns to teenage banter, with all its exaggeration and hopes. Gwen and Jim, Meg's parents, enter and Gwen begins to complain about the evening. She begins to attack Jim verbally over the lost keys. By the time Roy and Coral enter Gwen is ready for a Bex (headache powder).

Roy and Jim converse with Gwen interjecting complaints. She also tries to talk to the seemingly withdrawn Coral, but gets no response.

Harry and Vic, Tom's parents, enter full of life. The couples then begin to discuss their holidays. Harry and Vic are going camping in a lean to with the car. Jim and Gwen are caravanning and Roy and Coral are heading to the Gold Coast for a motel holiday.

The group disperses and Gwen talks down Tom's family. He hears her and gives a return speech full of anger and bitterness. Gwen just continues on until she stalks out.

QUESTIONS FOR ACT ONE SCENE ONE

- In this scene what do responders discover about the three family groups in the play? Create a chart showing their relationships. You could also comment on their different socio-economic status.
- What character traits has Gow established for Gwen?
- Describe each of the discoveries the different families are undertaking. Also indicate about how each one feels about the journey of discovery they are to undertake.

SCENE THREE

Coral gives a long, emotive speech about 'That boy' and ends in 'Alas' repeated. Roy comes in and the scene reverts to dialogue, but we know he is concerned about her. They exit together.

QUESTIONS FOR ACT ONE SCENE THREE

- How does Coral's mental state appear to the audience?
- How does Roy feel?

ACT TWO

SCENE ONE

Harry and Tom talk about their holiday back at their house but the conversation appears to be strained with fake happiness. Tom, at times, seems to be the one in charge. It is here we first hear about the 'hospital', indicating that Tom's sick.

Harry asks him to pretend to be happy for his mother's sake and they both agree.

QUESTIONS FOR ACT TWO SCENE ONE

- What have you discovered about each of the characters in this scene?

SCENE TWO

Gwen, Meg and Jim are preparing for their caravan holiday and Gwen is still complaining about almost anything that comes to mind. She has an occasional tirade and seems to take pleasure in making the others miserable.

Gwen leaves the room and Meg only half-jokingly asks her father if he wished that Gwen were dead. He asks her about her relationship with Tom and she responds reasonably. He explains to Meg why Gwen is a complainer and nag and similarly he too had it tough. He uses this to excuse her behaviour.

QUESTIONS FOR ACT TWO SCENE TWO

- How does Gow establish that the family is slightly dysfunctional and Gwen has real problems?
- How do you think this family feel about the coming journey?

SCENE THREE

Roy and Coral are talking about Coral 'behaving like a ghost'. He says she has become a liability to his career and life because of her inability to communicate and her withdrawn behaviour.

We find in Roy's explanation that they have lost a son in the Vietnam War and this has affected her. We hear how they are not the only ones and other arguments but they do little for Coral.

Coral says they 'need a change' and the journey for them means they will be able to get away from things and discover something new. He asks her to be like they were and she tries to respond but there is much doubt. The scene ends with Coral saying, 'We'll have a wonderful, wonderful time.'

QUESTIONS FOR ACT TWO SCENE THREE

- Summarise the problems between Roy and Coral.
- Research Kim Novak on the Internet. How is she relevant to the ideas in the play?
- The purpose of the trip for these two characters is to discover each other again and perhaps something about themselves. Do you agree with this statement?

SCENE FOUR

Tom and Vic are talking about their trip after they have woken in the night. Vic keeps apologising for the 'basic' type of holiday they are going on. She also talks about how Tom will get bored.

Again Tom is asked to act happy on the holiday in a near repetition of the conversation he had with his Dad.

QUESTIONS FOR ACT TWO SCENE FOUR

- Why is it so important that Tom try to be happy for his parents?

ACT THREE

SCENE ONE

This scene opens on Christmas Eve on the Gold Coast. The setting is the Gold Coast luxury hotel where Coral and Roy are staying. There is music and dancing. Coral begins to talk to a woman named Leonie but Coral is so intense and inquisitive she nearly begins to cry. Leonie keeps questioning her until she blurts out her husband is having an affair with a twenty one-year-old woman. She leaves distressed.

Rick, a young man, enters and tells Coral he is looking for his wife. He has had an argument with his wife over lunch and it is distressing as they are on their honeymoon. Coral tells him that she visits here every year and she knows most of the people at the hotel.

Rick tells Coral about his plans for the future and the National Service. The conversation strays to war topics and Coral thinks he'd be a 'good soldier'. Roy rushes in looking for her and they go off to dinner leaving Rick to wait for Susie.

QUESTIONS FOR ACT THREE SCENE ONE

- How does Coral scare Leonie?
- Why does Coral say at the end of the scene to Roy, 'I'm doing well aren't I'
- What impression do we get of Rick from his appearance in this scene?

SCENE TWO

The scene is in a caravan park where Gwen continues her barrage of complaints and criticism, even though it is Christmas Day. She and Jim begin to argue about a cardboard carton, where he has hidden her Christmas presents. They give the other presents with Gwen complaining until Meg accuses her of leaving the carton behind deliberately.

They argue hard and Meg tells of the Christmas game they play with the presents and how Gwen has wrecked it. Gwen talks about the order of things but Meg knows that she is right and Gwen has tried to sabotage the day. Gwen talks about hardship and then leaves to get a Bex.

Jim tells Meg what she was like in the early days of their courtship but then the campers arrive. The campers have formed a group and want to protest about conditions. They have organised a petition and want a priority system. They have organised a meeting and give Jim a list of problems. Meg and Jim remember when the holiday site was a simple place and he tears the list up.

QUESTIONS FOR ACT THREE SCENE TWO

- Why does Gwen deliberately leave the presents behind?
- How does Meg catch her out? What does this tell us about Meg and the relationship she has with her mother?
- The campers add a touch of humour to the scene. What other purpose do the campers have?
- Describe Meg's relationship with her father.

SCENE THREE

Back at the Gold Coast, Coral is talking to Rick on the roof of the hotel. It is obvious they have formed a relationship of sorts and he gets 'excited' when he sees her. He is beginning to question his life and then they disappear together into the dark just before Roy comes looking for her.

Roy calls to her and she and Rick come out from the shadows. Roy tells Rick to straighten up and he leaves. Roy threatens her with shock treatment and locking her up. She says she will think about it and then says she'll be fine.

QUESTIONS FOR ACT THREE SCENE THREE

- Why has Rick become obsessed with Coral?
- How does Roy show his frustration that she hasn't made any self-discovery and their relationship is the same despite the setting change?
- Compose a letter to a friend from either Roy OR Coral explaining the incident on the roof from their personal perspective.

SCENE FOUR

This scene is a huge storm where Gwen, Jim and Meg are driven away by the storm that seems stirred by the fairies. Gwen tries to save their material possessions, while Jim is worried about personal safety.

QUESTIONS FOR ACT THREE SCENE FOUR

- Gow uses the fairies in this scene and they remind us of the beginning and *A Midsummer Night's Dream*.
- For what other purpose are they used?
- What does this scene show about the two characters of Gwen and Jim?

SCENE FIVE

The storm has passed and it is a bright, warm day. Tom, Vic and Harry are on the beach. They are discussing what they will do with their day and how they had been lucky to have missed the storm.

QUESTIONS FOR ACT THREE SCENE FIVE

- Contrast this scene with the previous one. What contrasts do we see between the two families?
- What is the purpose of this scene?

End of Act Three

ACT FOUR

SCENE ONE

As Act Four begins Vic, Harry, Jim and Gwen are on the beach and Vic talks about the beauty of the beach. They all agree it is a beautiful spot. Jim tells of what happened to his family after the storm. After their van and other things were ruined they went to a motel but didn't enjoy it and went driving. Meg finds the beach.

It is time for the holiday camper's amateur night and Tom's family is getting ready for it. Coral enters and Vic, who has watched her behaviour, comments on how she sits on the rocks and stares at the sea for hours. Gwen goes off about 'mad people' who have no ambition. Vic takes her for a walk.

Jim and Harry talk about life and Harry tells of his migration from England and Tom's cancer. Harry thinks Tom doesn't know about it and gets Jim to promise he won't tell. The women come back and Harry and Vic leave for town to get things for the amateur night.

Gwen seems to be breaking down and she can't even take a Bex. She and Jim go for a walk to the water.

QUESTIONS FOR ACT FOUR SCENE ONE

- What has united the family groups?
- Describe Gwen's state of mind.
- Harry and his family have already had to adjust to the discovery of a new land, Australia from their English home. Now they have to adjust to the discovery Tom is dying.
- What have these discoveries affected the family?
- Compose a brief scene that involves the conversation that Gwen and Vic have on their walk.

SCENE TWO

Tom and Meg are talking about Coral and how she has escaped from her husband who is still on the Gold Coast. She has left him and hitched down the coast. Tom has recognised her as the Principal's wife so he says hello and she tells him the story. Coral has escaped so he wouldn't lock her up and she claims she is now feeling better.

Meg tells of how her family came to the beach. Tom then tries to get her to have sex with him as he knows he is dying and just wants to experience sex. He tells her about his illness and time in hospital. He gets her to promise she won't tell his parents that he knows he will die.

She still rejects him and they begin to talk about the amateur night concert. Meg leaves and Coral enters. Coral has gathered wood for the bonfire and Tom says they need more. She asks after his health.

QUESTIONS FOR ACT FOUR SCENE TWO

- How do we know that Tom and Coral have developed a relationship?
- Why does Tom ask Meg for sex?
- What has Tom discovered about himself through the course of the play?

SCENE THREE

The amateur night concert has begun and the MC (Master of Ceremonies) tells jokes and sings with crowd involvement. Tom appears as a sailor and tells of a ghostly sailor who meets a strange woman and they fall in love.

The woman, who is played by Coral, is turned into a mermaid but is saved by her love, the sailor. He tells her she must go back to her own people.

She walks off and the crowd applauds. The bonfire is lit and everyone leaves.

QUESTIONS FOR ACT FOUR SCENE THREE

- What is the role of a Master of Ceremonies in the production? Why does Gow have this role to open the scene?
- What is the purpose of the story of the sailor and the woman that he loves?

How is this story appropriate, especially for Coral?

End of Act Four

ACT FIVE

SCENE ONE

This scene is a silent one and it follows the playwright's extensive notes. Basically, Gwen gets her presents, Coral and Roy are reunited.

QUESTIONS FOR ACT FIVE SCENE ONE

- Why does Gow include this silent scene?
- What effect do you think it would have on an audience?

SCENE TWO

Back at the school, Miss Latrobe is preparing the class to read Shakespeare's *King Lear*. Tom reads the King's opening speech from that play to end *Away*.

QUESTIONS FOR ACT FIVE SCENE ONE

- Tom's speech from King Lear has relevance to his own situation. Describe that relevance.

Drawn & Etched by Robert Dudley.
CORDELIA. "SIR DO YOU KNOW ME."
King Lear. Act IV. Sc. VII.

SETTING

The overall setting of the play is in Australia in the years 1967 and 1968. The relevance of this has been explained in the context section at the beginning of this book.

The basic settings of the play are:

- School
- Harry and Vic's home
- Jim and Gwen's home
- Roy and Coral's home
- A Gold Coast luxury hotel
- A tent and caravan city
- The beach

It is worth noting that the indoor scenes occupy the beginning of the play while for the later scenes move outdoors. The list above is in chronological order and confirms this. Even the final scene at the school is outdoors.

It is this journeying outside that allows for the characters to transform themselves. They are taken out of their normal home environments and they journey to new destinations. This is amplified for Gwen and Jim who are taken away from even their regular holiday spot.

Gow is very general when he sets the scenes e.g. a tent and caravan city which gives the director a large scope for creativity. Likewise he doesn't give extensive notes in the play for the director and actors to follow. The settings are generally symbolic rather than specific and they represent the lives of the characters at first and then become new and threatening.

Payne writes in a review in the *Sydney Morning Herald* 12 June 1992 p16 that one production used multiple sets,

> *'Hoddinott has created a contemporary version of medieval mansion staging. Like the medieval audience we move from place to place. There are three raised platforms: one for the early school scenes, one for the home preparations for going away, and one for the uneasy, mostly unhappy, scenes when each of the families is first away. Then after the interval, we're seated around a sun-bright rectangle of sand.'*

Gow's theatricality allows this type of work to be done with his setting.

The storm is the catalyst that brings the disparate families together at the beach and Gow creates the fairies so it can be done on stage in a symbolic rather than literal way. The things that he is specific about are the music and lighting which he uses to create specific moods.

Gow uses the outside to allow characters their freedom. Coral for example is constantly upset and disturbed and can only change when she escapes and is given the freedom of the beach where she can sit and stare for hours.

Finally Gow allows the play to come back to its origins in the school. Both the characters and the set have been moved outdoors to reflect how the characters have developed.

CHARACTER ANALYSIS

- Tom
- Harry
- Vic
- Jim
- Gwen
- Meg
- Coral
- Roy
- Rick
- Leonie
- Campers

Tom

Tom is the main character of the play in terms of plot development. He is the figure that links the three disparate families in *Away*. The audience knows he is important from the opening scene when he has the stage to himself as the fairy Puck.

It is important to note here that in *A Midsummer Night's Dream* that Puck is a controlling figure in that he instigates much of the mischief. Here Tom seems to be more unifying and brings characters together at the end. He provides the opportunity for people to be united and he brings resolution.

Tom has his own problems to face as he is dying of leukaemia and probably has little time left. His parents have taken him on this holiday as nearly a final offering and both ask him to be happy so as to give the impression of normality. They are unaware that he knows he is dying.

The time that he shows his fallibility is when he asks Meg for sex, somewhat out of desperation, 'I want you to let me do it to you' (p49) Meg rejects his advances even though she is told his story. Fortunately they are both young and resilient enough for their relationship to survive this incident.

Tom helps Coral come to terms with her grief. At first she sees him as her lost son but later, at the beach, he has a conversation with her. He talks to her, 'I told her...well, I told her a thing or two that helped.' (p48) Tom is also the catalyst that helps Gwen. When she hears his story and sees the brave way in which Harry and Vic have coped she seems to lose some of her prejudice and accept new ideas, thus developing new attitudes to life.

Unfortunately while Tom helps heal other characters he has no such future. The last time we see Tom in the play he is reciting the first speech from *King Lear* where he says we 'Unburden'd crawl toward death.' (p57) This reminds the audience that Tom has finite time and won't have the happy ending of the others.

Character Quote

'They don't know. That I know. They want me to think I'm going to be right as rain. They mustn't find out I know. They mustn't even suspect, the poor bastards. And you won't fill them in.' (p50)

Character Questions for Tom

- Describe how Tom is coping with his illness.
- Discuss how Tom is the catalyst for the play.
- How do you think Tom helps Coral when they meet at the beach?
- Tom's relationship with his parents is positive. Why do you think Gow portrays it this way?

Harry

Harry is Tom's father and husband to Vic. He is not one of the central male figures in the text as he never involves himself in any conflict. He is avoiding telling Tom that he is dying and this remains the one untold secret in the family, 'He doesn't know. He won't know. We mustn't let him know' (p45). This gives the audience some good insights early as he and Vic ask Tom to be 'happy' for the sake of each other.

Harry is a 'New Australian', an English migrant who has come to Australia for a better life. He has no regrets and lives for the moment rather than planning for the future, 'We have no regrets, but we have no hopes' (p45). This is both a reflection of his life and the impending death of his son. He has left England after the war because he could see no future for himself or his family.

They are happy simply camping for a holiday and have no real expectations of anything more. Gwen is highly critical of this early in the play, 'They shouldn't be going on a holiday if they can't afford one'. (p11) But it is this family that shows resilience and makes it through in Gow's play. They seem to have the best life of all the families.

Character Quote

'We have no regrets. We don't get homesick. Only once a year. We book a telephone call to our old street. In Nottingham. We get out our old photo album. Remember for a while. But we have no regrets.' (p44)

Character Questions for Harry

- Why does Harry have 'no regrets'?
- What discoveries does he make through the play?
- What reason does he have for not telling Tom about his impending death?

Vic

Vic is Tom's mother and wife to Harry. Her name, reminiscent of victory, typifies her attitude. She is resigned to the death of her son and helps others come to terms with their lot in life. She has a very positive attitude to life and the problems it throws at her.

She is an English migrant who has come to a new country for a better life. She has adapted to this change and kept her positive attitude, even though they don't have much materially. She thinks of Harry when she tells Tom to pretend to be happy on the holiday.

Her positive and happy attitude seems to pervade the text. She always looks at the best side. She is an optimist; 'It's marvellous to sit' (p42) and 'You'll laugh till you're sick' (p43) are two examples of how Vic sees things. In Act Two Sc 4 she can still joke with Tom about the holiday and the Christmas presents despite her deep sadness at his illness.

She maintains this brave face and helps the other characters. While the others think Coral is mad she finds her 'an interesting looking woman' (p43) and helps Gwen after she has a minor breakdown on the beach.

While she materially has the least of all the women in the play she is far more balanced and accepting of life's difficulties and better adapted to dealing with them.

Character Quote

'It is a wonderful place. And what a piece of luck you found it.' *(p42)*

Character Questions for Vic

- Vic always seems positive. What life experiences would make her look at life like this?
- What do you think she helps Gwen by taking her for a walk? How does this helps them in their discoveries?
- What reason does she have for not telling Tom about his impending death?

Jim

Jim is Gwen's husband and the father of Meg. He is the 'meat in the sandwich' between Meg and Gwen when they fight. He genuinely loves both of them and tries his best to keep the peace in this dysfunctional family. Jim does not contribute to any of the conflict in the play; rather he is a conciliatory figure, 'Don't get upset'. (p8)

Jim has to walk a fine line in not alienating either Gwen or Meg as they both seem to be fighting for his affection. He defends Gwen against Meg's attacks but he has a better relationship with the daughter as we see in the camper's scene. He spends much of the play defending Gwen, 'Please don't be hard towards your mother.' (p17).

Jim has seen the better side of Gwen when she was young and they were struggling for survival. Jim says to Meg, 'Life was so much harder' (p18) but it hasn't embittered him as it has her. Instead he has adopted the role of accepting blame for all the problems just to get some peace. He is more than a 'hen pecked' husband as he sees more clearly than this narrow definition he is sometimes given.

There can be no doubt that he doesn't like the situation that he is in but he does the best he can to mitigate the conflict, at his own expense.

Character Quote

'My wife is not really an angry woman. She has high hopes.' (p44)

Character Questions for Jim

- Jim defends Gwen. Why does he do this despite her obvious problems?
- Describe his relationship with Meg?
- What does he discover about his family on their journey?

Gwen

Gwen is the wife of Jim and the mother of Meg. Gwen is a bitter and unhappy woman who has no enjoyment in life and tries to take enjoyment away from others. She is always critical and seemingly angry at the world.

Part of this stems from her early experiences in the depression and her internal drive to 'better' herself in economic terms. This motivation has left her emotionally hollow and her family is completely dysfunctional. She produces the most conflict in the play but is the most changed from her journey of discovery by the end of *Away*.

Her conflict with Meg is central to the play and this is how Gow shows much of Gwen's outlook on life. She talks of that kind of life, 'Motorbikes. Tattoos. Drink. A sad, dirty life.' (p11) She worries that Meg will take up with these kind of people and she will be lost. Gwen dislikes anything out of the ordinary and can't cope with change.

The pivotal argument between these two is the long argument in Act Three Scene Two when they argue over the Christmas presents. Here we see Meg fight back and her mother shows her ability to be cruel when she says to Meg,

> *'You're developing a nasty streak. A very nasty, cruel streak. You know what you're becoming? Snide. A nasty, snide girl. No one likes a snide girl, always arguing...Throw your future away. Give it away. Throw what I have done, we have done in our faces.' (p32)*

This argument also shows Gwen's motivations and she angrily tells Meg what they have done and she doesn't appreciate,

> *'Sacrificed! Gone without. Gone through hardship so what happened to us will never happen to you. So you'll never know what we saw- never, never, never... Isn't that something, miss? Tell me? Isn't it?' (p32)*

Gwen does not want Meg to have to suffer the hardship that she and Jim had to go through and this has made her narrow minded and insular. She can't even enjoy a holiday and never smiles. Her most common comment is 'It hurts. I need a Bex.' (p8) Her tight nervous state is manifested in headaches and she seems to live on Bex.

The audience knows that Gwen has changed because of her inability to take Bex near the conclusion of *Away*, 'I can't take this powder. I can't make it go in. I want to take it and it won't go in. I'm going to be sick.' (p46) Perhaps this is an indication that she will return to her less conservative youth when she had the courage to leave her parents.

Gow has portrayed Gwen as the typical nineteen-sixties housewife who was preoccupied with material possessions and quite snobby. Notice how she is extremely polite to Roy the Principal and Coral his wife but is initially dismissive of Harry and Vic because they are poor and work, 'In a factory, isn't it? (p11) She is also criticises their holiday, "A lean- to. They shouldn't be going on a holiday if they can't afford one.' Gwen thinks that their new van and possessions has improved their status.

This kind of attitude was prevalent in the sixties when life in Australia seemed easy. Gwen dominates her family with bullying and talk of a better life but she cannot emotionally connect with others because she is insecure. It is only when she is confronted by real loss, Tom's death that she can begin to see real loss and pain.

Gwen's physical journey brings her loss but with redemption. She has learned to face life again and we see her begin to be reunited with Jim. She even asks what he thinks, 'What do you think of me? You must hate me? Why do you still bother? I'm sorry... there are all these questions I want to ask.' (p46) This is a big change for Gwen and we now know she has the capacity to change.

Character Quote

'Everyone does what they have to. If we're to have any sort of reasonable holiday we're going to have to pay for it. We're paying for it now. (p15)

'Fun. Now there's a good word. Fun. It doesn't seem much fun.' (p15)

Character Questions for Gwen

- Describe the relationship between Gwen and Meg.
- Describe the relationship between Gwen and Jim.
- Why does Gwen try to spoil the holiday by deliberately leaving the presents behind?
- Do you think Gwen is justified in her attitudes and behaviour? Why/ Why not?
- Describe Gwen's journey after the storm. What changes occur as she discovers more about others and herself?

Meg

Meg is the teenage daughter of Jim and Gwen and she is the voice of youth in the play. She is very strong and she is able to stand up to her mother as we see when she confronts her mother over the Christmas presents being left at home. She will not be reconciled with her just for the sake of peace as her father is. She says clearly to her father, 'I don't think anyone should give in for the sake of peace and quiet.' (p18)

Meg is also strong, not just with her mother, but with the plans for her life and general attitudes. She does not have sex with Tom even after he tells her he is dying and she tells her Jim, 'I won't stay here forever.' (p17) She is used by Gow to typify the seemingly rebellious teenager of the sixties who does not have the conservative values of previous generations. The sixties were fertile ground for teenagers as economic conditions were good and they had the time to challenge existing views. Meg does this.

This is not to say that Meg is insensitive. She loves her father and mother and is kind and sympathetic to Tom on the beach. She has the strength of character to overcome his advance and still be friends. She even tells him hesitantly, 'it's just that...well... you're a bit skinny for me.' (p51) Meg is honest and open and is the new generation leading the way.

Even in the physical journey Meg leads the way. She is the one that takes them to the beach after the storm and insists they go down the dirt road. Jim explains this to Harry, 'it was the girl's idea completely. She...my wife, gave up. She was very upset. But the girl kept on at me. She didn't let up until we were on that dirt road. She's a handful.' (p44) Meg is the one who provides the place for them to regroup and be transformed.

It is interesting to note that in one version of the play Gow changed the ending to have Meg speak the final lines of the play on the beach rather than Tom at school. It provides a more positive end to *Away* and reinforces the transformation that has happened to the characters. While this is not the ending set for study it is interesting that Meg is seen as the character who has the ability to convey this message.

Meg is the future and she has a positive role to play. Her generation are the ones who will make the future and she is determined to do it her way. She is more self-assured than rebellious and her criticisms seem justified in the context of the play. Meg is the one who removes the carton off stage at the start of the last scene and this symbolises the removal of the old. We know that Meg will lead a different life than her mother.

Character Quote

'You worry too much' (p17)

Character Questions for Meg

- Describe Meg's relationship with her parents.
- How does Meg interact with the other teenager in the text, Tom?
- Make a list of five words that you can use to describe Meg.
- How does Meg contribute to the discoveries in the text?

Coral

Coral is the wife of Roy and the mother of a now dead soldier. It is the death of her son that has led to her breakdown as she doesn't seem able to cope with the grief of it. Her name suits the beach scenes with its sea connotations but also because coral was used by the ancient Romans as a charm against whirlwinds, storms, evil spirits and sickness.

Coral seems to search through the first three-quarters of the play for a replacement son for the one she has lost. She sees Tom as a possibility early but Rick becomes the focus of her attentions at the Gold Coast. By seeking the son she has lost she hopes to find her purpose in life and be the woman she once was.

Early in the play we see her unresponsive to Gwen's conversation and in Act One Scene Three she is outside and alone where she give a soliloquy where she finishes with how she feels, 'What's in a word they always say in those plays? Alas? [she sighs] Alas.' There can be no doubt that she has problems and it is hoped that the journey to the Gold Coast for the Christmas holidays will help her.

Before they leave she promises Roy' I'll be good! I'll improve. Watch me get better.' (p20) Unfortunately on the Gold Coast things don't improve from Roy's perspective and we see Coral create a distressing situation for Leonie although Coral seems sincere in trying to communicate. Her level of inadequacy is seen again in the way she is attracted to Rick, a boy the age of her son who has recently married and has escaped the draft.

Coral is over emotive as Gwen has no emotion. Coral cannot see the world through anything but the death of her son. She has no way of coping other than to mimic her husband's words and try to get along. She wants to get back to where things were and be like 'Kim Novak' for him but it isn't happening. Coral has lost the ability to have fun and her serious and broody nature make it difficult to be in public.

When Roy threatens her she runs away from the hotel on the Gold Coast and hitchhikes down the coast to meet up with the other characters on the beach. When she is introduced in this setting we see her thus [Coral enters in a flowing caftan, dark glasses and a huge straw hat over a scarf.] Vic sees her as an artist and says, 'isn't she an interesting looking woman? She's been here a few days now. She just arrived one morning all by herself.' (p43)

It is here, at the end of her journey of escape, that Coral finds redemption in the shape of Tom. He is the one who offers her words of advice and she seems to have accepted them. This is because Tom understands death better than anyone and he can show her the reality of acceptance. He says of her, 'She's been talking to people she said. She doesn't feel different to anyone else any more. I told her...well, I told her a thing or two that helped. She's ready to get back into the swim, she says.' (p48)

She performs in the play with Tom and copes with this public display well. We can see the bonfire as a symbol of her renewal to the world. In Act Five it seems that she and Roy have been reunited and they will begin again. They show such tenderness toward each other in this scene that we can only assume that they will be together happily in the future.

Character Quote

'Don't worry about me. You don't have to worry about me. I'm going to go to our room and I'll have a good think about what you said. I'll sort things out.' (p40)

Character Questions for Coral

- Describe Coral's problem and why Roy can't help with changing her attitude.
- Describe in two sentences the relationship between Coral and Rick.
- How has Coral changed in her journey down the coast to the beach?
- What does Tom do to help her?
- Is her reuniting with Roy a valid conclusion to their relationship in the text? Is this an example of rediscovery?

Roy

Roy is the husband of Coral and the Principal of the local high school. He is very determined in the way he faces the world and he cannot accept that his wife is having mental problems. He is uncertain how to help her and resorts to threats to bring the situation to a head.

Roy is the typical Australian male to some extent from the sixties. He has trouble proncuncing the ethnic names, 'and Mrs Papa... Papalapa...Papalax..oh well, I'm sure she knows who I mean, ha ha ha, for making the outfits.' (p4) We also see that he doesn't really appreciate the Shakespeare, 'When you said that bit about you have slumbered here you were certainly hitting the nail on the head. Not that I was bored.' (p9)

Roy does not show the same level of grief as Coral and he uses his position and responsibilities to focus his feelings. He tells Coral she should be more aware of these things but thinks the journey and holiday to the Gold Coast will help. It needs to be remembered that mental illness was not well understood in the sixties and Roy's reactions are typical of the time. Locking people away was a method of treatment and there was not any public sympathy or understanding for patients.

When he catches Coral on the roof with Rick he dismisses him and then threatens her, 'Look at me. I'll lock you up if that's what it takes. I'll keep you under lock and key if you insist. But you won't behave like this. You won't ever see another living person. You won't bother anyone.' (p40) He can't see any other way and he feels he needs to conform to public perception rather than let nature and time heal her grief.

He can't understand her public emotion and inner pain when he has coped. He tells her logically, 'We are not the first people in the history of the world to lose a son in war. There is a time for being grief stricken, there's a time for weeping and wailing and carrying on and beating your breast, but it comes to an end. It has to.' (p20) Roy needs this logic but it has no effect on the pure grief that Coral feels. Even though he doesn't understand we still feel that he loves her, even though he has threatened her. He still will 'come and visit' her and 'look after her'.

Roy does the best he can but it is only at the end in Act Five when they are reunited we see confused Roy reunited with Coral in a touching scene.

Character Quote

> *'Please, please stop doing it to me. I didn't send him. He had to go. Would you rather not pay the price for the life we have?' (p21)*

Character Questions for Roy

- Roy seems focused on his public image. Why is this so important to him? Think also about life in the sixties, attitudes and gender roles.
- What does Roy want Coral to do?
- Why do you think Roy finally threatens Coral on the roof of the hotel?
- What do you think Roy has come to realise by the end of the text?

Rick

Rick is the young man who Coral meets at the Gold Coast. He is there on his honeymoon, having just married Susie. The only character he interacts with in the whole text is Coral. He seems besotted with her although he is just married.

Rick seems to re-evaluate his life when he talks with Coral and he gives her what she needs, a son again. He says to Coral, 'I'm just going around the twist, I think. I do things I don't understand.

I have a job I didn't want. I got married and I can't remember why. I'm going to buy a house and I can't remember why.' (p39) He is the typical sixties young man who has lived life to meet the expectations of others.

When Coral runs from Roy we don't see him again in the text. It is assumed that when Roy dismisses him he goes back to Susie.

Character Quote

'But I get excited when I know it's time to see you again.' (p38)

Character Questions for Rick

- What role does Rick have in the context of the play?
- What do you think Rick gets from his relationship with Coral?

Leonie

Leonie is a woman whom Coral meets before dinner at the hotel on the Gold Coast. They strike up a conversation where the intensity of Coral scares her. She is obviously distraught by the conversation and desperately unhappy with her life.

Leonie seems to have all the material possessions, staying at the hotel 'every year' but she seems very keen to get away from Coral and cries, 'If you don't let me go I'll call for help.' (p25) Even under pressure she still pulls it together to go to dinner. She is another version of the unhappy housewife, albeit a wealthier one.

Character Quote

'My husband has been sleeping with a twenty- year old girl. I know where she lives. I want to kill her.' (p25)

Character Questions for Leonie

- What role does Leonie have in the context of the play?
- Why does Gow only allow Leonie to interact with Coral during the play?
- Is Leonie a realistic character?

Miss Latrobe

Miss Latrobe the English teacher has only a small role in the text but it is important. It is important because she explains to the class (and audience) why King Lear is worthy of study because it shows the transitory nature of life and also deals with human nature. She talks of the power of nature and we can reflect back to how the beach and water seems to have healed the characters.

Lear is searching for eternal truths as we all are and when she lets Tom take the part of the dying King she lets us know that much has been learnt and also lets him see his own fate clearly. She is also a reminder that literature does offer something to audiences.

Character Quote

'it is the struggle between man and nature, as well as between man and man, and between man and himself that make this for me, his masterwork.' (p57)

Character Questions for Vic

- Miss Latrobe prefers *King Lear* to *Hamlet*. Why does she prefer *King Lear*?
- Do you think this scene is superfluous as many critics have suggested or is it integral to your understanding of the text?

Campers

The campers appear [A clump of campers comes in] and they represent the conservative, bigoted view of Australia. They do provide some much needed humour after the conflict in the argument between Gwen and Meg. While this satirical parody is funny it has a serious edge in that they echo Gwen prejudices and intolerance in a more public way.

They want to make the campsite just like the homes they left, 'They should feel right at home while they're on holiday.' (p35) They show their prejudice when they discuss the migrants at the park, 'They're not bobbing around in the Mediterranean now' (p35) and 'the New Australian campers might need to be reminded of the way proper Australian families run a holiday.' (p35)

They even have plans for nature in their drive to claim the campsite with their 'beautification' plans. They are organising more rules and a petition. These small-minded people are treated with derision by Gow and he even has Jim reject their small mindedness by tearing up their list.

Character Quote

'we're also a little concerned about some of the people who've started putting in an appearance over the last few years.' (p35)

Character Questions for the Campers

- What role do the campers have in the context of the play? What do they show about some Australian attitudes in the sixties?
- Describe the humour and why Gow makes this scene humorous.

Fairies

The fairies appear in the opening scene of the play, [Kids dressed as fairies scuttle about in garish light], and they again appear in the storm scene, [The fairies return and stage a spectacular storm].

Gow uses the fairies to represent the magic in life and the possibilities that nature provides in its magic. They seem to have acted upon Tom's curse.

> *'I hope you have a rotten holiday. I hope it rains. I hope the dunnies overflow and you all get the runs. I hope you get sunstroke and end up in hospital. I hope all the fish you catch are poisoned. I hope you have a fucken miserable time.' (p11)*

This storm allows Gwen to be free of her possession such as the caravan and head off better prepared for the change to come.

Character Questions for Fairies

- Why do you think Gow has the fairies in the play?
- Research the role of the fairies in Shakespeare, particularly *A Midsummer Night's Dream*. Do the fairies in *Away* mirror their role in that text?

THEMES

- Discovery
- Discovery through Journeying
- Change as an Agent of Discovery
- Nature and Discovery
- Discovering Relationships

Discovery

Discovery is our main concern when understanding *Away*. I am sure you have studied the rubric and analysed what discovery is so I will examine here and in the following sections how discovery can be analysed in terms of *Away* as a drama and also by individual characters. You should keep in mind that *Away* is a piece of theatre and when you consider discovery it is vital that you discuss the theatricality which is how the playwright allows the audience to discover his ideas. Obviously the audience discovers the play as it unfolds in terms of content and development of ideas and characters but it is integral to your response to think about it in terms of what we see not just the words that we read. For example we discover much in Act Five Scene One where there is no dialogue yet Jim and Gwen discover they have a bond despite what has gone on before and Roy and Coral seem to have commonality and reached a tacit agreement based on what we see. This is all about theatricality and discovery through movement and space on stage.

Away is also about discovery in that people discover much about other people and about themselves. The journey that they embark upon gives them the space and opportunity to meet each other afresh, in a new setting and shake individuals out of their routines and behaviours. Miss Latrobe sums up the idea of discovery when she says at the conclusion of the play,

> *'It is the struggle between man and nature, as well as between man and man, and between man and himself...'* Act Five Scene Two

Meg, for example, learns much about her mother and the family's early domestic situation which enables her to deal more constructively with the situation. Coral tries to re-engage with the world by escaping and self-analysing yet it is not all introspective. We learn about people and prejudices through the campers and their activities in the play. Also revealed are the secrets people keep through the different circumstances that, once discovered, create both positive and negative emotions. For example the revelation of the woman when pestered by Coral,

> *'My husband has been sleeping with a twenty-year old girl. I know where she lives. I want to kill her. I'm going to have my dinner now. With my husband. Don't speak to me again'* (Act Three Scene One p25)

is especially negative in the context of the woman's life and the situation yet the revelation of Tom's impending death by Tom to Meg and by Harry to Jim have different effects. It is wise here to consider how the discovery of a secret can have varying effects. It has changed the way that Harry and Vic see the world and how they plan for the future. It is interesting that they keep the discovery of his impending death secret from Tom but he too tries to protect them from discovering the truth even though he uses it to try and convince Meg to sleep with him so he can discover sex.

As mentioned previously, the idea of place is also useful to acknowledge as it provides the opportunity and acts as a catalyst for change. One example is Roy and Coral's trip. As Coral tells the woman at the 'Gold Coast Luxury Hotel',

> *'We've never been to Queensland before. We usually tried to all go somewhere overseas for the Christmas holidays. Last year we didn't. We got a house by the sea. I was a little worried about coming to such a big place. There are so many people staying here.' (Act Three Scene One p23)*

Yet the best example of place allowing discovery is the beach where all the characters end up after the storm. Here the disparate families come together and resolutions are reached and discoveries made that change how characters see each other. Here secrets are revealed, new relationships forged and the concert takes place. As we have learned many of the characters have issues and Coral sums this up best when Roy tells her to 'come back to reality' and she replies,

> *'I mightn't like it there' (Act Two Scene Four p20)*

Gow also shows us in *Away* that the discovery of an individual's motives helps us and other characters comprehend why a character acts as they do and creates an empathy with them that leads to understanding and the change discussed earlier. Jim tells Meg of Gwen's difficult past, we learn Coral has been damaged by her son's death in the Vietnam War, Tom's leukaemia has altered his perceptions and those of his family while Rick is struggling to adapt to married life and the expectations of Susie. By discovering why people act the way they do we can relate to them more clearly and the outcomes are better received, especially in a performance setting where you don't have the time to reflect as deeply as you are now.

Think also that discoveries can be minor things such as the lost keys which nearly cause Gwen to have a meltdown or the unifying force of giving the Christmas presents left behind in the cardboard box. We see this in Act Five Scene One,

> *'Jim comes in with the cardboard carton. He takes out a parcel and hands it to her. She unwraps it. It is a pair of slippers. She looks at them, then at him and walks away, a bit overcome. Jim goes to her and they embrace.' (p56)*

I have already discussed the significance of the finding of the beach but little things can have a major impact. Finally before we move into more detailed analysis in the following sections I would like to mention discovering imagination and relate this to the concept of Shakespeare and the fairies. This relates to the concept of theatre that I began with and the suspension of belief when you enter a theatre. Theatre requires you to discover and part of that is an imaginative journey, a thought worth keeping in mind as you discover *Away* for yourself.

Discovery through Journeying

The physical journeys that the characters undergo transform them from their initial state to a state where they can better interact with the world. On these journeys they gain self- knowledge and to some extent inner peace by discovering much about themselves and others.

The pattern of the journeys as illustrated on the following page is quite straightforward. The journeys begin at the school, move to the family homes and then move to the holiday destinations. The families are drawn together by the events of the play and all end up at the beach where more discoveries are made. After the changes that occur there they journey back home, their lives changed through the discoveries they have made on the journey.

The holiday is usually seen as a time of renewal but until the families break the cycle they are behaving in exactly the same way they do at home, it is like discovering a new way of life. It is when they journey to a new place that renewal through discovery occurs. It is positive and effective.

The journeys in this play are not just the literal physical journeys, although these provide the impetus to discovery, but the figurative journeys that the characters take i.e. the personal or self-discoveries.

The basic pattern of the journeys in the text is:

The dream-like start at the school

The family homes

The holiday destinations

The beach

Back home to reconciliation and a renewed life.
We see Tom at school

These holiday journeys provide not only a change of scene but a chance for renewal and a chance to grow. Some characters' discoveries result in a more tolerant and understanding attitude.

Gwen is a good example of this. She realises that her materialistic values are not as important as she thought. To come to this understanding she must face Tom's death and how his parents have coped. At the end of Act Four Scene One she says to Jim, 'No. let's walk. Come on, down to the water. The water's so warm'. (p47) This symbolic purification allows her to develop and cast aside her snobby prejudices. Her discovery leads to personal change. Coral too just needed to get away and break free from the pressure that she was under because of her grief. All the character's journeys allow them to develop personally through discovery. Roy becomes reconciled to Coral, Gwen and Jim can begin again and perhaps even recapture the fun they had as young people together.

Another physical journey that has been mentioned is that of Tom's struggle with leukaemia. Here is a discovery that isn't so positive one that takes him from from health to sickness and one that won't go away. It is interesting to see how Tom approaches and comes to terms with his illness. We know that he is scared but he helps the characters either through direct conversation or by admitting the fact that he is dying.

May-Brit Akerholt writes in the introduction to the play, '*Away* is essentially about coming home, or undertaking a journey from ignorance to knowledge; from blindness to insight.' (pxii) This change through discovery can only be undertaken with a journey to a different place. These journeys of discovery play a vital role in *Away*.

Theme Quote

'Shhhh Roy... Shhhh, relax. We need a break. A rest. Rest and recreation. Let's get away. Just the two of us.' (p21)

Theme Questions

- Take each family group in the text and create a flow chart of their specific discoveries. Make a point of describing the major change at each one.
- What qualities does the beach have that makes the journey there so worthwhile in terms of discovering self?
- Why do you think Gow has the characters travel home at the end of the play? Do you think this is essential to the text?

Change as an Agent of Discovery

Change in *Away* is usually driven by Tom who is in the play to 'restore amends' or set things right between characters and within themselves. It is this self-change that occurs most commonly in the text and it is the discoveries that characters make that give them the chance to change and fall under Tom's influence.

A good example of this is Gwen who changes from being a manipulating, over stressed wife and mother to an individual who can see that life is not about control but about understanding. It is finding out that Tom is dying and there is nothing anyone can do that begins her change. This is cemented in her walk with Vic and her conversations with Jim on her return. For Jim she may have come full circle as he talks about her before she became stressed as a person with humour who was full of life.

Coral is another character who changes through the text. She has a number of personas. She begins as the grief-stricken housewife and mother who cannot cope with life. On the Gold Coast she develops a relationship with Rick in an effort to be 'normal' in the eyes of society and Roy. At the beach she plays the role of an artist and finally is transformed by her performance with Tom in 'The Stranger on the Shore'. At the end of this play within a play she walks away to return to her life with Roy where she belongs. We see them reconciled later in the play.

Roy has also changed from a socially and position focused man to a more understanding person in Act Five. His insensitivity is stressed by his threats to lock Coral up and use shock therapy on her. This makes their reconciliation all the more meaningful.

Meg is another character who changes considerably from the intolerant girl of the opening scenes to the more accepting and forgiving young lady we see at the end of the play. She has changed due to her contact with Tom and his story but also because her father has shown her positive things about her mother. By the end Meg seems to have changed enough to be accepting of her family.

Gow views personal change as a positive thing but not so the change that the campers want. This is sarcastically portrayed and he mocks their attempts to be racist and environmentally destructive.

Theme Quote

'My wife is not really an angry woman. She has high hopes.' (p44)

Theme Questions

- Choose one character in the text and describe the change that they undergo through a discovery and what effect this has on the people around them.
- What purpose does Gow have in showing the change the campers want negatively? Compose a list of the changes they want. Is this a negative discovery?
- How is the theme of change affected by the presence of Tom in the play?
- What role do the fairies play in the changes that occur?

Nature and Discovery

Nature plays a significant role in the text and part of the healing process is the fact that the characters end up on the warm, sunny beach that goes for miles and miles. This healing power of nature helps with the regeneration and restoration of the characters.

For example Gwen goes for a walk with Vic and has a symbolic paddle and comes back a changed woman. She then says to Jim later, 'Come on down to the water. The water's so warm.' (p47) Coral spends hours staring at the sea before her healing and in the short play at the concert she is metaphorically immersed in the sea.

Nature can also be cruel before it heals and this is shown through the storms. The storm in Act Three Scene Four is the climax of the play and it completely changes Gwen's life. The storm also ties in with the idea of the Shakespearean devices in the text.

Shakespeare's plays used the storm or tempest to show inner turmoil in a character and in this text the storm reflects the emotional turmoil in the families that Gow is exploring. Nature destroys Gwen's material possessions and without this destruction she could have never come to terms with what is really important in her life.

This storm is shown on stage and is described as, [...the fairies who wreak havoc with noise, light and frenzied activity.] This destructive force is also unifying as it drives the characters to the one point and then becomes a benign force.

Theme Quote

'There didn't seem to be much point in carrying on after that washout. There doesn't seem to be a reason to carry on with your holiday when your van's a wreck, your boat's smashed on the rocks and all your clothes are soaked.' (p43)

Theme Questions

- Imagine you are Meg. Describe the scene at the caravan park in your diary the day after the storm has wrecked your van and boat. What do the characters discover about themselves and others in a crisis?
- Why does Gow use the fairies to convey the impression of the storm on stage?
- Discuss the use of water as a cleansing and healing force in the text.

Discovering Relationships

Discovering relationships and the ability to communicate are core themes in *Away*. In the text we have three families who just can't communicate honestly with each other due to either social or emotional pressures. While Vic and Harry's relationship with Tom seems sound they cannot bear to tell him the truth about his illness.

The other two families seem totally dysfunctional and they have little idea of communication or how to develop relationships. Gwen rules by decree and incessant bullying while Jim just accepts his lot and tries to hold back the tide. Meg is not so easily controlled and she goes on the offensive making for a household in constant conflict.

Roy cannot understand Coral at all and has no understanding of the depth of her grief at the loss of their son in the Vietnam War. She has lost all her social skills in her withdrawal and he cannot see her in any other way than in terms of how society perceives her. It isn't until the shock of her leaving that he comes to any realisation about their relationship.

Gow also gives the audience the teen romance but it is also not quite what we have come to expect. Meg is her own woman and rejects Tom's clumsy advances despite his story about the illness. She is adept at maintaining their relationship within her own terms, despite her parents ignorant worrying. While they reconcile as friends there can be no romance.

All the other couples relationships seem to be reconciled at the end of the play because of the discoveries they have made. Vic and Harry seem to have done theirs prior to the play as they have had a few crises in their lives but Gwen and Jim and Roy and Coral form the group that are regenerated and go on to better things in their relationships.

Gow shows that relationships are about people not material things and also about listening and acceptance rather than bullying and making demands.

Theme Quote

'When you're married to someone do you ever wish they were dead?' (p17)

Theme Questions

- Take each family group in the text and create a flow chart of their relationships. In one word describe the relationship each character has with each other at the end of the play.
- What contributes to the improved relationships between the couples at the conclusion of the text?
- Compose a report that analyses Gow's views of relationships using quotations from the play *Away* as evidence in your report.

LANGUAGE

Away combines a variety of language techniques to impart its character and thematic concerns. Obviously with a play the dialogue is of supreme importance and much of the dialogue is conversational and colloquial. Webby writes in *Modern Australian Plays* (1990 p 55) that:

> *'Away combines basically naturalistic dialogue with a theatrical form that persistently reminds the audience it is watching a play rather than 'real life'...there are numerous scene changes and a wide range of interior and exterior locations, all suggested schematically rather than in naturalistic detail.'*

Gow uses the dialogue between the individuals in the families and also the conversations between families to convey both character and plot. The conversations are realistic in that they portray how Australian families related to each other in the sixties. Much of the personal angst displayed is still universal in families forty years on and this keeps the play relevant to modern audiences.

A good example of this is the bitter dialogue between Gwen and Meg. This type of exchange, the battle of the generations, will be fought out forever. When Meg says, 'I won't stay here forever' she echoes the thoughts of thousands of teenagers searching to discover their own identity and place in the world.

Gow doesn't just dwell on the negatives of family life and the characters are capable of showing great love for one another. Harry and Vic show great love for each other and Tom and Jim shows love for both Gwen and Meg. Families tend to make for emotive language as the conflict comes from knowing each other too well and the issues which are important and raise passions.

Gwen shows the cost of these emotional battles by constantly taking headache powders and others lead their lives on the edge. Gow portrays this through bitter dialogue such as Meg's, 'When you're married to someone do you ever wish they were dead?' (p17)

Contrast this dialogue with the banter between the two teenagers, Meg and Tom, especially in the first Act. This kind of banter is very natural between teens as they find themselves and their relationships. They hedge around the important issues with trivia and make light of serious situations.

When discussing language you also need to consider the effect of Gow's use of Shakespeare through the text. This seems to bring a more formal and theatrical feel to the text. Shakespeare is instantly recognisable to most audiences and opening the play with the speech from *A Midsummer's Night Dream* gives the play instant appeal and alerts the audience to the idea of escape.

The speech from *King Lear* to conclude the play and the final line 'Unburden'd crawl toward death' gives the play a strong conclusion and focuses on the human condition. While death is inevitable, it is a choice to be burdened or unburdened.

LANGUAGE QUESTIONS

- Describe the importance of the use of the Shakespearean plays in *Away*.
- Find three examples in the text that show Gwen's character clearly.
- How does Gow show the audience that he is mocking the campers? Give two specific examples from the text.
- Create a list of emotive terms used in the dialogue between Gwen and Meg. How do these terms add to the conflict in the text?
- Do you think the dialogue between Meg and Tom is realistic? Support your response with specific quotes from the text.

THE ESSAY

The essay has been the subject of numerous texts and you should have the basic form well in hand. As teachers, the point we would emphasise would be to link the paragraphs both to each other and back to your argument (which should directly respond to the question). Of course, ensure your argument is logical and sustained.

Make sure you use specific examples and that your quotes are accurate. To ensure that you respond to the question make sure you plan carefully and are sure what relevant point each paragraph is making. Topic sentences are helpful to begin each paragraph and it is solid technique to actually 'tie up' each paragraph by linking it to the question.

When composing an essay the basic conventions of the form are:

- Address the question, state your argument, outline the points to be addressed and perhaps have a brief definition.

↓

A solid structure for each paragraph is:

- Topic sentence (*the main idea and its link to the previous paragraph/ argument*)
- Explanation/ discussion of the point including links between texts if applicable.
- Detailed evidence (*Close textual reference- quotes, incidents and technique discussion.*)
- Tie up by restating the point's relevance to argument/ question

↓

- Summary of points
- Final sentence that restates your argument

As well as this basic structure you will need to focus on:

Audience – for the essay the audience must be considered formal unless specifically stated otherwise. Therefore, your language must reflect the audience. This gives you the opportunity to use the jargon and vocabulary that you have learnt in English. For the audience ensure your introduction is clear and has impact. Avoid slang or colloquial language including contractions (doesn't, eg, etc).

Purpose – the purpose of the essay is to answer the question given. The examiner evaluates how well you can make an argument and understand the module's issues and its text(s). In the case of the Area of Study, markers look for a deep conceptual understanding and you must reveal understanding using examples from your prescribed text and a related text or texts. An essay is solidly structured so its composer can present ideas with clarity. This is where you earn marks. Essays do not retell the story of a text or state the obvious. They analyse rather than describe.

Communication – Take a few minutes to plan the essay. If you rush into your answer it is almost certain you will not make the most of the brief 40 minutes to show all you know about the question. More likely you will include irrelevant details that do not gain you marks but waste your precious time. Remember an essay is formal so do not do the following: story-tell, list and number points, misquote, use slang or colloquial language, be vague, use non sentences or fail to address the question.

HSC STYLE ESSAY QUESTION

Remember that essay responses must respond to essay questions and when you submit a practice essay, it should have a question written at the top. Start by underlining the key words in the question.

The Concept of Discovery may be conveyed differently in and through texts, but the result for responders is a deeper understanding of self and the world.

Discuss this statement with close reference to your prescribed text and two related texts.

PLAN

Introduction Start by introducing the texts you are using in your essay response ***Argument:*** The BOSTES definition for Discuss is to -Identify issues and provide points for and/or against. Consider using differing textual forms which affect how the concept of Discovery is conveyed. For example, a film will convey the concept of Discovery using visual, filmic techniques whereas a novel will use narrative techniques. Using a variety of textual forms will enable you to argue for the first half of the statement and enable you to show the different ways discovery is conveyed. Also consider the rubric and reflect on the different ways Discovery can be and is presented in your texts.	You need to let the marker know what texts you are discussing. You can start with a definition but it can come in the first paragraph of the body. You MUST state your argument in response to the question and the points you will cover as part of it. Don't wait until the end of the response to give it!

Do not forget the second part of the question, that is, the link to you as a responder and your deeper understanding of self and the world, through studying Discovery. You may like to argue that although forms and text types differ and aspects of Discovery raised in and through texts differ, it is this variety which helps you as a responder relate the concept to your own understanding of the world and your place in it.

- (Aim to incorporate discussion of techniques when discussing text and making close textual references.)

↓

Idea 1– Look to the rubric and identify what kinds of Discovery are raised in your texts.

Idea 2- Explore how these are raised, through selected form and relevant techniques.

Idea 3 - Analyse their impact in terms of discovery on you as a responder. Is it a bildungsroman text. Do characters make personal discoveries, grow and learn? Is the composer him or herself a factor linked to a responder and discovery? Look at the purpose in writing the text. Explore these ideas in both your prescribed and related text or texts. In what ways have the aspects of Discovery raised in the three text enhanced your understanding of yourself and the world?

Ideas can be expanded into several paragraphs. be sure to set out paragraphs clearly using a topic sentence, explanation, examples and analysis of examples in terms of technique and link to question.

↓

Finally, your conclusion should incorporate a summary of key ideas. Do not raise new points in a conclusion.

- Provide a final sentence that restates your argument

Make sure your conclusion restates your argument. It does not have to be too long.

DISCOVERY: SUGGESTED RELATED TEXTS

You are often advised to select related texts that do not mirror the form of your Prescribed text. In addition, you are reminded to select related material wisely and look for links to the rubric, the concept and to highlight similarities and differences with prescribed material. Markers have noted that the judicious selection of related material is a key factor when evaluating responses. Sophisticated texts when well analysed in relation to the concept, and strongly analysed in relation to the prescribed text, will impress markers more than texts you may have happened to read at school in previous years in Stage Four or Five.

In the following list, categories are used for convenience but titles are not always exclusive to genre or text type. Many hybrid texts exist which cross boundaries of genre.

PROSE-FICTION/NON FICTION

Bypass – The Story of a Road by Michael McGirr

About one man's journey of discovery along the Hume Highway between Sydney and Melbourne. This is a hybrid text which is part travelogue, memoir, history and romance.

Gulliver's Travels by Jonathan Swift

This classic tale is about Gulliver's discovery of Lilliput. Through his arduous adventures he discovers lessons about society and humanity. The tale is a satirical view of the state of European government, and of petty differences between religions. It addresses the origins of human corruption, the conflict between Lilliputians and Yahoos, and other races.

A History of Reading by Alberto Manguel

Discover a personal response to books and reading and a love of literature. This is a wonderful non-fiction text written by an award winning author.

Looking for Alibrandi by Melina Marchetta

The aspect of discovery here is Alibrandi discovering who her estranged father is, as well as coping with various teenage issues in high school. This text is not as sophisticated as some other choices but it does raise aspects of culture and personal discovery.

Memoirs of a Geisha by Arthur Golden

This novel is about personal discovery and the development of identity in a tumultuous period in Japanese history.

The Secret River by Kate Grenville

Discover the interaction between the white settlers and the Aboriginal population on the Hawkesbury River. The discovery centres on place, people, including the composer, and cultures.

Small Island by Andrea Levy

Told by four narrators, the novel is set during the Second World War and tells the story of four different lives. There is racial tension and discovery of what it is like living with someone who comes from a different part of the world. Not only do you discover this new way of life, but it brings about a discovery of the self.

***So Much To Tell You* by John Marsden**

Here a scarred and introverted girl who is an elective mute, discovers a way to reveal her feelings to the reader in the form of a diary. In turn, readers discover Marina's life and relationships as she also discovers non-verbal ways to communicate with others.

***Unpolished Gem* by Alice Pung**

In this text the Discovery theme involves cultural differences, migration and a new life for an Asian family in Footscray, Victoria. This text is about discovering life in a family and about cultures.

***An Unsuitable Job for a Woman* by P.D. James**

Female detective Cordelia Gray investigates a suicide and a family with many secrets. The writing is detailed with plenty of atmosphere and clues. It is a crime fiction text, detection discovery with a twist. Consider other examples of Crime writing as discovery is a key theme within this genre

***The Snowman* by Jo Nesbo**

Detective discovery in a European setting. This text presents modern take on the genre and is very well written.

FICTION / FILM

Alice in Wonderland (novel and film) original by Lewis Carroll

Alice discovers a magical fantasy world where she is in turmoil. Here she has amazing adventures and meets many intriguing characters.

Chronicles of Narnia (novel and film) original by C.S. Lewis

Four children, Peter, Suzan, Edmund and Lucy, discover a magical world behind their wardrobe and learn about their special role in saving the land from a great evil. The form of allegory can help responders discover deeper truths.

The Lost Thing (picture book and film) original by Shaun Tan

A boy discovers a lost thing and journeys to find it a home.

The Never-ending Story (novel and film) original by Michael Ende

The protagonist Sebastian discovers the world of Fantasia which is dying. He becomes part of the book he is reading and saves the world.

Sherlock Holmes (novel and film) original by Conan Doyle

Any of the *Sherlock Holmes* mysteries of adventures such as *The Hound of the Baskervilles* are recommended. These texts present discovery through means of deduction, calculation and scientific reasoning.

Under the Dome by Stephen King (novel and film)

Imagine being trapped and cut off from the world under a dome of power. This is a Science fiction text that is a long read but an intriguing idea. The initial discovery is awesome but then characters begin to discover things about themselves and others.

Where the Wild Things Are (picture book and film) original by Maurice Sendak

A young boy is punished by his mother to go to his bedroom, which transforms into a jungle where he sails to an island and discovers that it is inhabited by malicious beasts known as the "Wild Things." After successfully intimidating the creatures, Max is hailed as the king of the Wild Things and enjoys a playful romp with his subjects. However, he discovers that being king is not all that great. If you select a Picture book, be sure to discuss visual literary techniques in a sophisticated manner.

Wizard of Oz (novel and film) original by Frank L. Baum

Dorothy discovers a magical fantasy world where various characters discover their true character. For example, Tin Man finds his heart.

The Book Thief by Marcus Zusak

A young orphaned girl meets her new family in Germany during the Second World War. Through the focalisation of this young girl the reader pieces together the narration and discovers what is going on in the world around her. Historical discovery.

FILM

The Island directed by Michael Bay

Science fiction film about clones that live in a false utopian prison who discover their true origins as spare organ parts for wealthy but terminally ill people. The revelation is the discovery and how the discoverers respond to it.

It's Kind of a Funny Story directed by Ryan Fleck

A teenage boy checks himself into the mental ward only to find he has been relocated to the adult's ward. The film follows the boy and the friends he makes along the way.

50/50 directed by Jonathan Levine

Adam learns how to cope and live his life by coming to terms with his cancer.

An Education directed by Lone Sherfig

Jenny is in her final year of high school and has high hopes for the future when she meets a middle aged man who shows her another world. Jenny has to decide which world she wants to live in.

Consider also documentaries and other non fiction filmic forms.

POETRY

A suite of poems rather than one single poem is recommended, especially if the poem is brief.

'Easy Does It' by Bruce Dawe

A poem about discovering his boy and how he has to be 'careful' with him.

'Discovery' by Wislawa Szymborksa

The poem begins with 'I believe in the great discovery' and it is about faith and evidence.

'La Belle Dame Sans Merci' by John Keats

A knight discovers a new love and a new faery world but it is not what it seems and his discovery in this poem leads him to a life of misery.

'My Last Duchess' by Robert Browning

A dramatic monologue which reveals chilling and disturbing details about the speaker.

'Spring and Fall – To a Young Child' by Gerard Manley Hopkins

This is an address to a young girl, Margaret, and raises the discoveries that the child will make about the human condition. There is a prediction that these discoveries concerning life and death will be inevitable and with come with age and maturity.

SONGS

Remember that, if you write about a song, you are advised to consider more than just the lyrics.

At Seventeen by Janis Ian

Teen coming of age song about the angst of discovering what and who you are.

Kings and Queens by 30 Seconds to Mars

Discovering empowerment and greatness from despair.

Meant to Live by Switchfoot

Making the most out of life and discovering your absolute potential.

We Won't get Fooled Again by The Who

The persona in the song discovers that the new government which is established after a revolution is the same as the old government, and criticises it.

WEBSITES

100 Questions to Inspire Self-Discovery

HTTP://WWW.ALEXANDRAFRANZEN.COM/2013/04/18/100-QUESTIONS-TO-INSPIRE-RAPID-SELF-DISCOVERY/

Quite a few sites like this one that offer ideas on the topic. Read judiciously.

Discover the Extreme World

HTTP://WWW.MILESKELLY.NET/PRODUCTS-PAGE/DISCOVERY-EXPLORE-YOUR-WORLD/

Read the book blurb: Produced in association with Discovery Channel, this jam-packed book focuses on the extremes of core reference subjects. From animal giants to futuristic spy technology to the deepest caves and coldest places in the Universe. Nice change as it is aimed at children.

Discover Magazine

HTTP://AU.ZINIO.COM/MAGAZINE/DISCOVER/PR-500621662

Science based but has a wide range of articles on all sorts of interesting topics such as foods and environment.

HTTP://WWW.MILESKELLY.NET/PRODUCTS-PAGE/DISCOVERY-EXPLORE-YOUR-WORLD/

Discovery channel

HTTP://WWW.DISCOVERYCHANNEL.COM.AU/

Here you will discover many shows about discovery but it is also about learning.

Discovery Education

HTTP://WWW.DISCOVERYEDUCATION.COM/TEACHERS/

This address will lead you to the teacher resources but the site is full of content that shows another aspect of discovery i.e. education.

Famous People who Made Scientific Discoveries

HTTP://WWW.BIOGRAPHY.COM/PEOPLE/GROUPS/DISCOVERY/SCIENTIFIC

Another excellent source for evidence in film and written form on a comprehensive site.

Kids Discover

iPad app. Below is the address for the preview but you can download the app and use it. Excellent resource.

HTTPS://ITUNES.APPLE.COM/AU/APP/KIDS-DISCOVER/ID574832964?MT=8

The Science Channel

SCIENCE.DISCOVERY.COM/FAMOUS-SCIENTISTS-DISCOVERIES/100-GREATEST-DISCOVERIES.HTM

Almost complete collection of all the scientific discoveries covering most of the ancient and modern worlds in film and clearly explained.

Self Discovery

HTTP://EN.WIKIPEDIA.ORG/WIKI/JOURNEY_OF_SELF-DISCOVERY

Here are some definitions and links to the topic. A useful starting point to develop your ideas.